STRENGTH

Words by Harlan Wade

Concept and illustrations by
Denis Wrigley

RAINTREE CHILDRENS BOOKS
Milwaukee · Toronto · Melbourne · London

Library of Congress Number: 77-7634

1   2   3   4   5   6   7   8   9   0   81   80   79   78   77

Printed and bound in the United States of America.

Library of Congress Cataloging in Publication Data

Wade, Harlan.
    Strength.

    (A Book about)
    SUMMARY: Text and illustrations demonstrate how
things can be strong on one occasion but not on another.
    1. Strength of materials — Juvenile literature.
2. Force and energy — Juvenile literature. 3. Muscle
strength — Juvenile literature. 4. Senses and sensation —
Juvenile literature. [1. Strength of materials]
I. Wrigley, Denis. II. Title. III. Strength.
TA407.W29   500   77-7634
ISBN   0-8172-0984-0 lib. bdg.

STRENGTH

The bridge
is strong,

but not strong enough!

This man is strong.

This man is not.

Some people can lift
heavy things.

Some people find it hard.

What is strong?

It takes a strong leash

to hold this dog.

It takes
a strong rope
to lift this
heavy elephant.

It takes a strong horse
to pull a heavy load.

It takes strong legs
to run fast.

Strong smells travel
on the wind.

19

He has a strong
liking for candy,

but a stronger liking
for ice cream.

Strength depends on
what has to be done.
This man's eyes are
strong enough
to see the paper.
But they are not
strong enough
to read the words.

The jug is not
strong enough to
keep from breaking
when it falls
to the floor.

A strong motor
makes the boat go fast.

The plant is not strong
enough to stand by itself.
It is tied to a stick that
is stronger.

The chair is strong enough
to hold the cat.
But look what happens
when the man sits down!

We wish to thank Mr. Glen Burk, Principal,
Wisconsin Avenue School, Milwaukee, Wisconsin,
for his assistance. We would also like to thank
Mrs. Gardenia Limehouse and her third grade class
and Mrs. Camille Maduscha and her second grade class
for reading some of the books in this series
and sharing their comments with us.

Lisa, age 8 — "The book was real neat!"
Melissa, age 7 — "I like the funny pictures."
Manuel, age 7 — "The book makes me laugh."
Eric, age 7 — "The story made me feel happy."
Julie, age 9 — "The size of the pictures is nice."
Johnny, age 7 — "There are neat colors in the book."

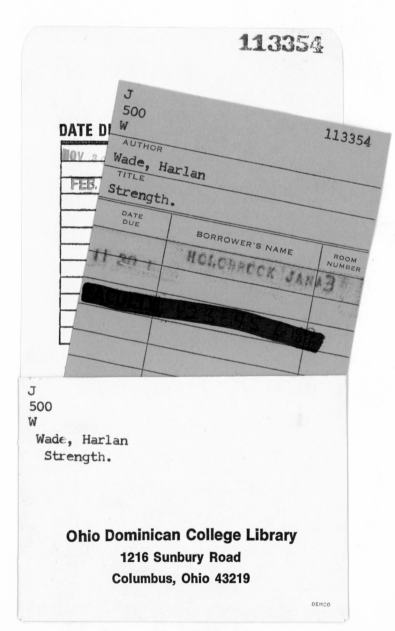